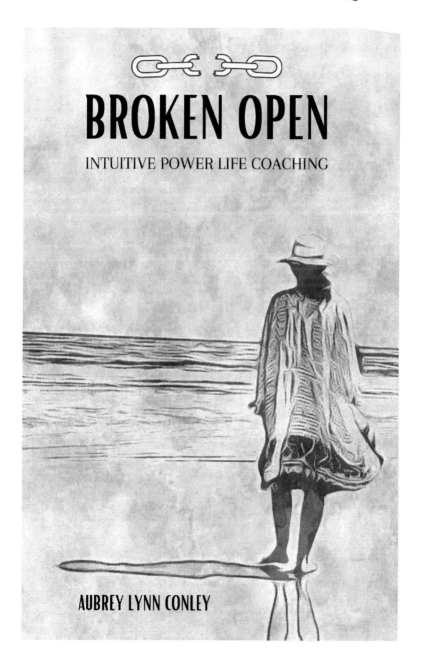

BROKEN OPEN

INTUITIVE POWER LIFE COACHING

AUBREY LYNN CONLEY

This book is offered to provide helpful information on the subjects discussed.

©2021 by Aubrey Lynn Conley
AUBREY CONLEY : L I F E C O A C H www.aubreyconley.com
Self-Published in the United States using BookBaby

ISBN: 978-1-09838-756-3

DEDICATED TO HUMANITY

May each human being find their inner voice, truly know themselves, friend themselves, love themselves and believe they are capable of choosing their own path.

AUBREY LYNN CONLEY

TABLE OF CONTENTS

AURORA

~Luminous - Roman Goddess of the Dawn

Broken Open is about finding that lifeline and relationship of strength *within yourself* - your *'soul-self'*.

You will come to know that no matter what is happening around you, you WILL be able to get through it.

I was at a time in my life where it felt like my world was falling apart. My extended family had broken up.

I am a Momma of two little kids, a wife, an entrepreneur. I am a sister, a friend, a cousin, niece, daughter, granddaughter and boss.

I am a mentor to many children and adults and - *everyone* wanted something from me. Though living in many joyful moments during this time- I was emotionally drained.

Then, my daughter's ongoing health crisis took a huge turn and I dropped to my knees.

At that moment, I felt very unsupported by so many people who I expected to step in, help, show up and love me and my family. I was so consumed with internal sadness that I just wanted to take my little family of 4 and our 2 dogs and move to an island somewhere to avoid the chaos surrounding these unsupported feelings and confrontational relationships that engulfed our lives.

I slowly realized as I journeyed through these life traumas that I was being "shaken" by the universe to widen my lens. This whole time, without realizing - I had been working, practicing and creating a different reality through everything I was being put through: for myself, my family and my relationships.

I developed the ability within myself, learning to tap into this sacred space that helped me seek shelter in my storms. But when I *finally* embraced my soul-self - MY reality, everything in life got easier, simpler, and those energy soul suckers that would show up from time-to-time in my life, eventually detached, too.

You will find that the balance of your inner *'soul-self'* will support and guide you to continue to live your life - day by day - through joy and love!

Following this discovery, I've found within myself the ability to move forward through life with love, happiness and joy - no matter what fell in my path.

I want to share my revelations with you.

Chapter 1

ONENESS

Do you ever have moments when you question your life's purpose?

> *Why am I here?*
> *What is this all about?*

Do you sometimes feel a profound calling to rise up and act, to do *something*, but you are not sure what to do or how to act on that feeling?

What if you had the ability to tap into your very own 'soul-self,' to center and realign? To start again from a neutral space with pristine clarity and a wider lens?

When I say 'soul-self' I mean that my mind, body and spirit are fully in sync on a neutral level- in an unbiased space- to act, speak, think and emotionally respond purposefully.

Sounds great, right? **But...** it takes a whole lot of practice; it takes enduring let-downs; it takes: "many try-and-try-again."

I still get pushed off the track some days. However, I'm not afraid of falling anymore, because I've learned how to pick myself up, and start again. I rely on myself in those moments; only *I* can change the direction of the course of *my* life.

There are preconceived thoughts each of us have developed through our lives. I refer to these thoughts as an "already, always-knowing".

Through this quest for a deeper connection within myself, I have realized there are no coincidences in life and that "luck "is not a thing. People are not lucky or unlucky; they are blessed or stressed based upon the realization of the "already, always-knowing" within themselves to see and speak their truths.

I discovered an incredible power I hold within myself; I also came to the realization that this power exists in each of us. By looking inward, using the gifts of insight and expanding my perception layer upon layer, I've learned the most valuable relationship I will ever have is the friendship I have with myself.

It has driven me to recognize the choice I have each day to lean confidently into living in a space of love, self-assuredness and happiness, with high energy and at a positive vibrational level. While I have the choice of how I want to feel, live and be in the moment, I also have the ability to heal my physical and mental health and wellness throughout my daily journey.

With practice, this discovery is available to everyone, at any given moment in each day. I needed to take a closer look in the mirror in order to know who I was, what I wanted, and how I wanted to feel in order to start my journey. You are going to have to go through this yourself, of course.

But I'm here to get you started.

There are going to be statements and verbiage you may not grasp or understand when reading the first time around.

Come back and reread it. Sentences and chapters will speak differently to you the second...or third... time around... This all starts with _you_ - right here, right now. By picking up this book you have committed to your own personal self-growth journey.

Having a relationship with yourself is the most important and utmost valued connection you will ever have with anyone on this earth. Learning to truly and fully love ... you ... is _the_ game changer.

Identifying and knowing your wants, likes and dislikes will be brought to the forefront of your everyday mindset. When you know what you want, you can attract those "wants" more easily; avoiding any drama and getting right to the point in a loving way.

"Showing up" as the best version of ourselves - in our careers, in our friendships and parenting, with our lover - will attract that universal "like" match, too.

Discovering your true identity and the greatness of who you are will allow you to pour onto others ... and yourself ... in ways you never imagined.

That's when the perfect unity within begins.

You may currently be choosing to just accept the way your life is and any chaos that surrounds you, stuffing those negative feelings, storms and beliefs way-down into your stomach, until one day you finally _implode_. Or, the exact opposite can occur if you _explode_, affecting others around you.

This doesn't need to be your "normal," or the way your life is "supposed to be." **You** get to choose to stop fighting against the ongoing current reality happening in your life and create the one you want.

You can start by searching for inner peace and practicing daily mantras and methods of your own. By leaning into those inner whispers and listening to your intuition, you won't ever have to hear your body scream.

Listen up friends, I have crawled through the mud, been at my lowest of lows, had hardships, was broken-hearted and even more. I have felt my body scream.

I have made the choice not ever to feel that way again.

Uniting with your 'soul-self' (which we will learn more about in future chapters) will become second nature. And the best part is..._**everything**_ in life becomes easier!

New paths will suddenly open and things will begin to always work out for you, over and over again. Once on this journey in full practice, you will see that even in stillness and times of uncertainty, growth is occurring. This process only works with consistency, commitment, coaching and education.

Being committed to your personal self-growth is the only way you will propel yourself to **whom, where** and **how** you want to be.

Remember friends, we *GROW through what we GO through.*

When things get hard, don't give up - **RISE UP.**

My vision for you upon completion of this journey of self-discovery is that you **choose to love yourself**; you need to dive in with both feet and seek out the things that set your soul on fire.

I can only speak of the journeys I myself have walked. I got to where I am today by exploring myself, listening more, speaking less, reading and following people I admire, like: Gabrielle Bernstein, Mel Robbins, Jon Gordon, Rachel Hollis, Zig Ziglar, Esther Hicks and Brene Brown, just to name a few.

I also got comfortable with being uncomfortable and that propelled my growth!

I am always seeking positive qualities from those in my tribe; those in whom I believe and see value in their supportive energy and guidance. The wise, the real; those whose *voices* aren't afraid to give and take constructive criticism. Those who aren't offended or afraid of *me* stepping into my best self.

Most importantly, I am living through my own experiences in life and *learning* from them. Investigating details, feelings and emotions deeper inside of me than ever before.

In order to do so I had to learn the art of *falling in love* with myself. It truly is an art, like a beautiful dance or musical vibrational connection you might have with a song.

It's how we learn what our <u>own</u> 'love language' is and teach others how to treat us and love us, by the way we treat and love ourselves.

Through this soul-self journey you will begin to figure out what I identify as your 'love-language': how you want to be treated, loved, and cared for. Your "love-language" will help you communicate to others how you wish to be treated.

I share *my* self-growth journey in hopes that it will be a key piece of **your** <u>toolbox</u> to empower you.

≫→ LET'S BEGIN!

Chapter 2

BREAKING THE CYCLE

We've learned behaviors and beliefs based on how we were raised. When you started living on your own, outside of your childhood home, did you gravitate toward purchasing the same cleaning products that your family cleaned with? Did you cheer for the same team your father did in sports events? Probably yes, because it was comfortable and what you knew.

Before we jump into the nitty-gritty, I want you to take note: there are many twists and turns that will take place along your personal self-growth journey. Remember, this is a journey not an overnight stay. This is not for temporary gain, or for short-term moments of joy; though you may feel some butterflies along the way.

The guidance in this book is for your end-game, your long-term, future self-of-tomorrow, for the next day, and for the decades after that.

The changes you make today do not just benefit you. They are also to set forth an open path for your children and your grandchildren.

Cleaning out old wounds is part of your self-growth journey. Facing your fears, limiting beliefs and maybe even revisiting some unkind corners in your heart and mind.

I am not a therapist; I am an Intuitive Power Life Coach. I am here to redirect and support you in starting where you are in life today.   I am *hopeful* that after reading this book, you will continue your personal self-growth journey by seeking additional growth opportunities.

Take a peek into your past and make a choice to break negative cycles that may be holding you back from living YOUR BEST LIFE. Without you even realizing, these cycles could be pulling you further from where you want to be.

Repeated cycles include old habits, fixed mindsets and negative behaviors. These patterns may have been passed through generations of family, through toxic relationships with family members, friends and past romantic partners.

> *Think: TOXIC - harmful to your mental or physical self-being.*

Can you think of behaviors that you share with generations before you? Does sounding like your parents and grandparents at times ring a bell? Whether good or bad, we are pretty much programmed since birth, through the influence that we fell into and the way those before us "think" things are supposed to be.

BUT ARE THEY?

Maybe you really _don't_ want to do those things or act some kind of way, or go to an event, but you sacrifice your own happiness because you feel bad or pressured by others.

That space of feeling uneasy, unsure or just not good is when you're disconnected from who you really are.

There is no instruction manual on parenting. We might think that others have the "perfect family life" - been brought up with unconditional love, spoken kindness and excellent guidance.

We may feel we were not brought up in that "ideal" environment, but it is ok to break away. It is "ok" to decide that we may want something different for ourselves and our own families.

Are you with me? If not, don't worry! You are about to have one of the most profound _"Aha!"_ moments.

How do we break a recurring cycle that is woven into our veins? How do we give ourselves permission to take back our sacred power - to *choose again* and lead our own lives?

We need to create a friendship with ourselves; welcoming a conversation of *who* we really are, identifying our personal wants, needs, desires and even more.
Each of us have internal triggers embedded inside our bodies from our past.
When that trigger sets off, something usually explodes negatively. These things follow us into our relationships with lovers, friends, our careers, our children and most importantly, with ourselves.

Breaking a cycle is hard, but you will find it to be one of the most beneficial and liberating steps you will take throughout your personal self-growth journey.

As we grew up echoing the relationships that surrounded us - parents, siblings, grandparents, friends, aunts and uncles - our ego was very much impacted on how to act and how not to act. Who to like and who not to like.

We were influenced in both positive and negative ways, because those surrounding us were our role models.

So, how can we break away from any of the negative influences that we continue to carry with us through adulthood? Acknowledging the negatives can be a really scary place to visit - but it can also be a lifesaving, refreshing thought.

When you form a loving relationship with yourself, the bravery gained will push you forward. Your kindness towards yourself will speak volumes and your understanding of self-connection alone _will be enough_ to navigate your journey and open that fixed mindset.

I want to share this passage with you. When it was first presented to me a number of years ago, I felt sad and did not agree. But as I traveled on in my life, I realized the truth in this passage and how we are affected by the generations before us. How important it is for us to gain an understanding of our sacred place of being an individual.

On Children

And a woman who held her babe against her bosom said, Speak to us of Children.
And he said:
Your children are not your children.
They are sons and daughters of Life's longing for itself.
They come through you, but not from you.
And though they are with you yet they belong not to you.

You may give them your love, but not your thoughts,
For they have their own thoughts.
You may house their bodies, but not their souls.
For their souls dwell in the house of tomorrow, which you cannot visit, even in your dreams.

You may strive to be like them, but seek not to make them like you.
For life goes not backward nor tarries with yesterday.
You are the bows from which your children as living arrows sent forth.
The archer sees the mark upon the path of the infinite, and He bends you with His might that His arrows may go swift and far.
Let your bending on the archer's hand be for gladness;
For even He loves the arrow that flies, so He loves the bow that is stable.

-Written by Kahlil Gibran, author of The Prophet

Establishing a relationship with ourselves outside of perceived expectations - how we *think* others think we should be - is crucial to our survival and overall happiness.

No one can feel what *you* feel or walk where *you* have walked. Only *YOU* can do that.

How good would it feel to know that you will always have yourself to count on, to do things <u>on</u> purpose, <u>with</u> purpose and because you want to! A delusion we all fall into is that there isn't enough time here on earth to do the things it really takes to accomplish all the goals we have. Stop worrying about our time here on earth and start seeking freedom from fear and stress.

> *Choose to speak on purpose, act on purpose and*
> *feel on purpose.* WOW! re-read that again.

Take 10 steps back and look around. Step outside of yourself for a few moments and take a look at the life you are living.

> *Is it intentional?*
> *Are you thinking for yourself?*
> *Are you kind to yourself?*
> *Are the thoughts you're thinking "your thoughts" or*
> *are they the voices of others?*

LISTEN to **your** thoughts, keep a positive mindset and speak your truth.

For so long, I felt my throat was closed and my voice box was stuck in a vise. I could not put my thoughts into words and speak them from my mouth. At times, I literally felt frozen. I could not wrap my mind around what my heart was trying to say, but I knew from the depths of my soul I had <u>so many</u> unspoken truths to speak!

At the time I was so unhappy with pieces of my life, down to my career and the business I started from the ground up. This place I created I once was so proud of and brought me joy.

Not even realizing it, I started my personal self-growth journey when I was willing to look inward.

I stopped looking at everyone else as the problem and started looking at my current self, my behaviors, the choices I made and those who I allowed in my circle to influence my decisions.

Who my friends were, what type of people I was attracting, including clients and those with whom I was doing business.

*I had allowed myself to be manipulated and stopped living intentionally from who **I** was, what **I** wanted and what **I** set forth to create for my life and the lives I impacted. I was emotional all of the time; felt like I was unbalanced and I recognize now that I didn't know my 'soul-self' - and guess what??? I didn't like it very much!*

EVERYTHING started to open up and life itself began to get easier once I recognized narcissistic people, negative patterns and my own bad habits that I felt trapped in.

⇒It's like I woke up.

This process was painful at times, but it also supported me to "own up" to my mistakes, the self- sabotage and harm I was

*doing and most importantly...to take a <u>good look </u>at **myself** in
the mirror.*

*Those people and places were removed from my life, and some of
those even included family and close friends. (God removes
people from your life because He hears how they speak of you
behind your back).*

Take a quick look around you. Do the people who are in
your everyday life feel like sunshine? Do you feel warm,
protected and positively influenced by them? Do you feel
love? Not just "some of the time," but ALL. THE. TIME. ??

When you get up from the table you share with family and
friends - there should never be whispers of cruelty or spite,
only love and adoration.

This chapter could turn into its own book. There is so
much information to be covered on this topic, we will
barely touch the surface.

The takeaway from this chapter is just this: start your
journey by surrounding yourself with positive people.

If you have a parent that pulls you down, put up
boundaries. Boundaries are necessary for healthy
relationships to thrive and grow.

If you have a "Negative Nelly" or unsupportive friend that
makes you feel exhausted - you feel badly after talking to
them, or they always see the negative and push "their way"
or how things should be in your life - put up boundaries
and get a little distance.

In order for you to see where you want to be, you need
some space to connect with yourself. I believe putting up
healthy boundaries between you and those who are in your
village will *in turn* bring you closer together.

Mark my words: *those who rise with you, crawl through the trenches - continuously showing up, and follow you to the sun without question, will become your tribe.*

HOW DO YOU START?

You start by listening more and speaking less.

Zone-in on your feelings and widen your lens when doing things; look at your habits and those you choose to spend time with.

Be prepared for people to walk with you on this journey and cheer you on with encouragement through your trials and triumphs. Recognize there will be those who will *not* like this inward change you seek due to their own thoughts and beliefs.

> *If you're thinking of negative interactions with people relative to your job or career, hang in there. Once you have been empowered by connecting to your soul-self- you will be able to interact with those you may not want to from a different view.*

This method, this book **Broken Open,** is for everyone; yet, some may not be ready to walk this path for themselves. Taking a look in the mirror and really owning up to who you have been to yourself and others - in thought and action, is challenging.

The goal at the end of your journey is to be so completely yourself, that everyone else feels safe to be themselves, too.

> **"Be the change that you wish to see in the world."**
> — *Mahatma Gandhi*

Chapter 3

YOU DESERVE TO BE WHOLE

"Live your best life!"

We hear it all the time, it's one of those trigger phrases. But really, how do you do that in everyday life?

We can take Caribbean Vacations, trips to Disney, go to the best restaurants in town, ride horses, ski the Rockies and hashtag be #livingyourbestlife on Instagram, all while loving the joy IN that moment.

These are examples of things that put us "temporarily" in a state of joy. #livingyourbestlife as an experience was probably pretty incredible. But, wouldn't it be pretty awesome to live at that level, that high frequency and vibration of love, happiness and joy <u>every</u> <u>single</u> <u>day</u>?

*I don't know about you, but I want to be able to
LIVE in JOY as much as humanly possible while I'm*

*here on earth. I designed a life I love. Vacations
now are for exploration, discovery and
reconnecting, but never to "get away."*

*I do believe a change of scenery and experiencing
new places is good for your soul: lovely, exciting
and it's also a chance for growth opportunities.*

*I choose to live with an attitude of gratitude every
single day, even on those dark rainy, cold days - to
keep my vibrations high and know that at <u>any</u> time
I'm able to realign inward, back to my center and to
a level of pure joy.*

Have you ever reached the top of the mountain you dreamt about? In your career, relationship, goals or any kind of success? Once you've arrived, are you looking for what's next?

Living in alignment with who you are and what you want, will keep you open to continued growth, success and a blessed life.

If you feel a void you can't seem to fill within yourself, the relationship between you and you is missing.

All the shoes, handbags, vacations, home upgrades or cars will never fill that void. They may feel good for a while, but you will continue to come back to that place of emptiness inside.

When you continuously come back to that pattern of living, those are **repeated lessons** given to you from the universe. If you are back where you started in a sense, you didn't learn the lesson at hand.

Try to see the silver lining in EVERYTHING and most importantly know that investing in a relationship with yourself comes first in all of this.

This is the most important and valued connection you will ever have with *anyone* on this earth. You literally need to live with yourself for the rest of your life! Why not live it fully, lovingly and centered - knowing you can always count on, rely and fall back on you.

BE KIND TO YOURSELF

Let's journey on to learning more in the next chapter.

Chapter 4

ALIGNING WITH ONE'S SOUL-SELF

"To align...to bring something into a straight line, or an easy agreement."

Imagine a chiropractic visit. The chiropractor adjusts your spine, neck, shoulders etc. to allow the body to connect, flow and work to its highest potential - mentally, physically and spiritually. To ALIGN.

This brings me to think immediately of my seven chakras. Do you know what your 7 chakras are? LEARN them.

The 7 Chakras are an important tool you will use to connect your physical-self with your soul-self. Each Chakra has a unique intention. This will help you have a better understanding of what is happening inside of your body, as you learn to live at an incredibly heightened vibration of clarity in life. This may come to you in small packaged moments, or snapshots, but prepare to continue to build upon those profound bits of *"Aha!"s* as they move you to the next level.

Imagine the burden on your physical body when your 7 Chakras are *not* in alignment.

That weight manifests itself through illness, headaches, not feeling well - both physically and emotionally.

SEVEN CHAKRAS

CROWN — wisdom, understanding

THIRD EYE — intuition, perception

THROAT — communication, creativity

HEART — love, compassion

SOLAR PLEXUS — power, will

SACRAL — relationships, vitality

ROOT — grounding, survival

Photo Credit: Pinterest: La Vie en Orange | korijock.com

Here is a great picture I found on Pinterest that provides a quick understanding of your Chakras.

Use this Space to Create a More Specific Meaning for Yourself in Practice

CHAKRAs	=	MEANS TO ME:
Root	=Grounding, Survival	
Sacral	=Relationships, Vitality	
Solar Plexus	=Your Power, Your Will	
Heart	=Your Love, Compassion	
Throat	=Communication, Creativity	
Third Eye	=Intuition, Perception	
Crown	=Wisdom, Understanding	

I'm not taking you into a yoga class or meditation lesson just yet. Stick with me, that comes later.

Let's talk about what I like to call our 'soul-self,' aka our spirit guide, that gut feeling, inner-voice sometimes referred to as your intuition.

You've read this 'soul-self' word and are probably thinking, what is that?

I use the word '*soul-self*' to describe the deep connection I discovered and I hold within *myself.*

First, I recommend you surrender any fixed mindset or assumptions, and continue onward with optimism and an open mind.

Second, be ready and willing to widen your lens and remember these lessons are tools to better your future self in all aspects of your life. Prepare to learn new things, indulge and step outside your comfort zone for opportunities to become centered, aligned and connected to Y O U R S E L F like never before.

Picture an imaginary straight line running through your body from head-to-toe, ***centering*** your every moment, feeling and thought - "everything on the same page" - TOGETHER at the EXACT SAME TIME.

Your SOUL-SELF is: your humility, spirit, thoughts, peace and compassion; mentally and physically united together evenly; with integrity, in a self-controlled, self-sustaining, positive, and inward space: always open to receiving more positive influence and light. A space that exists and can thrive inside of yourself. It is an ever-evolving process.

A space where **pure tranquility** lies and our **truest of truths**
are found. It is where y*our ideal balance* lives; existing and
ready to be tapped into.

The "*already, always knowing* "that we can count on
ourselves to fall into this space of thinking, feeling, being
and neutralizing -
> in *any* situation
> > at *any* moment
> > > at *any* given time.

This soul-self-awareness heightens the *growth of wisdom*
within you to *strengthen* and *enhance* the communication
with yourself and with others. You become attuned to your
inner voice.

This is an opportunity for our bodies to fully work the way
they were designed to: our 'whole-self' and *'soul-self'*
operating at full capacity, together, in love and joy; never
in mental exhaustion.
(This is a challenging concept, stick with me.)

If we want to experience daily happiness and move
through love and joy - recognize this high ***positive***
vibrational space is possible in any chosen moment. In
order to get connected with your soul-self, you need to
break away from negative impacts of society.

Imagine you are drinking a glass of the cleanest, purest,
yummiest water running through your entire body, from
your head to your toes. Feel that water flow through your
veins. Envision every single cell inside of you receiving that
cool, crisp, life-giving water.

As the water moves through your body, begin to form fresh
thoughts, new ideas, find inspired creativity to manifest
your wants from this new, refreshed and awakened space.
An *incredible* space!

And trust me when I say, once you get a taste of this sweet spot, it is life-changing!!! It will change each and every conversation you have with yourself AND with others.

Most of us are not connected to our soul-selves, but hear those whispers from time to time. We have gut feelings to turn right instead of left. We can become extremely emotional and overwhelmed in even the quietest moments.

Sometimes we feel pulled toward something that has propelled us in a better direction.

It's right there. It's that space between the subconscious and conscious voice inside ourselves; the things we question or feel reserved about are the things we should explore even more.

SO - back to those Chakras.

Recognizing the importance of lining up those Chakras to properly communicate and work together for your mental and physical well-being is crucial.

> *Prior to _my_ "soul-self journey," my take on being in alignment was very different from my understanding of the _flow of alignment_ that I hold within myself today.*

Remember, your soul-self-discovery is an on-going journey. I _continually_ have to practice; to make this process a part of my daily routine to stay connected and grow.

Like many things in life, the process of finding your soul-self is hard. It will take some commitment. It requires determination and perseverance to push yourself into the direction of self-love.

Totally worth the investment!

Chapter 5

BLOSSOM

"...to bring out the capabilities or possibilities of"

WHO ARE YOU?   What are your *real* likes and dislikes beyond the ingrained timeline that has influenced   your mind?

Can you answer that question confidently?

Think back to your childhood and the first set of memories you have. You were given an identity the day you were born.

But - who are you really? What makes you - you?

We are connected through humanity, although each of us holds unique talents, individual truths and a purpose to be here on earth.

No one of us is like the other. Not even identical twins. We each have our own soul-self.

We have been influenced every single day of our lives by our surroundings, mentors, television, radio, social media and so much more. At times our lives may feel like a tug of war.

We've been taught what to do, how to do things, what to believe in, how to act and even how to speak and respond - "tell Mary you're sorry" - even if we did not feel that way.

We have adapted to the guidance we were given growing up - both positive and negative.

> It is generally believed that by the age of 7 we have developed an association to love and relationships that formed through connection, conflict, intimacy and communication. All of this has been wired inside of our brain.

But, what about our bodies and our souls?
Who are YOU really?

I believe we are impacted by the yes-no-right-wrong (no in-between) "no-grey-area" of teachings and training.

Think back, recognize and start to visualize your thoughts. By following in the footsteps of those before us we have done what they did without even realizing it!

☞ REALLY THINK ABOUT THIS CONCEPT!!

We have many repeated cycles and yet so many _**unlearned**_ life lessons that were missed along our paths. This is being human and has been totally accepted by humanity.

It's normal right? Or - _**isn't**_ it?

If you took a step back and watched your life from the outside looking in, what would you see?

Would you _see_ life lessons and silver-linings that were right in front of you? Did you miss signals and signs from the universe - SCREAMING that you are not aligned with who you ideally and truly are?

Guidance influences our character. Learned behaviors, trauma, unhealthy relationships, healthy relationships are all passed down versions of what we have been taught life "should be" and the "expectations" others have of us.

Think about comparing ourselves to others. It is a negative approach that may have influenced our choices and behaviors. Recall the first time someone told you that _you should or should not_ do something a "certain" way.

This was _their_ opinion, but in that moment, we saw it as a direct reflection of ourselves being _right_ or _wrong._ That's when the _innocence_ of our natural, childlike space (where joy, imagination, creativity and love is held) went out the door. The moment you second-guessed your intuition and began questioning your likes and dislikes, your looks, your style, your path - without realizing it... you slowly changed.

You changed to align with how you thought others saw you. Even if you really *liked* what you were doing in that moment, even if it made you feel good - you changed for someone else's approval, validation or acceptance.

Have you *censored* your personality and behavior in the company of another - thinking it was more important to "keep the peace," please or make them happy?

Once you learn how to correct your fixed mindset by uniting with your soul-self (through friendship with ones-self) YOU can pass down these effective teachings and positive practices to future generations. Opening the skies through which future humanity will soulfully soar.

YOU will have the tools to help them discover who they truly are by finding their own soul-self. You can guide others to nurture the seeds of their youth's soul, mind and body.

THIS IS EMPOWERMENT

Celebrate your imagination! When random ideas and creativity show up - like daydreams - embrace and lean into them: step into that space.

Be aware of physical cues - like that fluttering sensation (I refer to them as joyful "heart flutter" moments). Your childlike intuitions are still there and they will inspire you to see things in a new light. I can promise you that.

We all have these blips and moments. We may not recognize it, but we experience these feelings and these moments of what I like to call HIGH vibrational space - "good vibes." We experience it when our high vibration of JOY sets in. Hold onto that feeling.

> *I believe we were put on this earth to live in joy, love and to give back to humanity, to each other positively. NOT hardship, struggle, jealousy or self-destruction. I believe the mind is an extremely powerful tool we can use to connect within a whole lot more than we think we can.*

Let's start forming our *own* thoughts and help others form their own, too.

Imagine the positive effects this will have on our world once you begin to use your inner-guidance and support of your own soul-self: that's when the "ripple effect begins".

The continuous spread of your self-revelation, empowerment and connectedness with your spirit will flow naturally. It will fill you up and you will unconsciously be affirmatively pouring onto others. Having a safe, nourished and loving relationship with **yourself** sends positive vibrations.

SELF-LOVE SHOULD NOT BE SO HARD

If we were taught "self-love" from the beginning of time - *the "already, always-knowing' how to connect our soul-self alongside our human-ego-self and LOVE ourselves at all times.*

Then maybe we wouldn't have to experience the pain of inner doubt, worry, body-shaming, jealousy, envy and so much more that negatively impacts our daily mindset.

We should never be envious of the love or relationship others may hold for another.

Life is not a competition or a popularity contest.

*I promise you - there's **ENOUGH LOVE** in this world:*
for you to love yourself and others;
for others to love you back;
and
for others to love others, too.

We don't need to define, quantify or place boundaries on these "loves" - each is unique (sister, friend, son-in-law, grandchildren, co-worker).

Understanding our own *love-language* will help us **blossom**; to love ourselves and to love others freely.

Chapter 6

HUMBLED

Think about the people in your life who fill you up, make you smile and feel whole. Those you depend on, care for and love deeply. Those who may even be a direct lifeline, voice of reason, guidance and support for you.

What would you do if those people were completely ripped out of your life tomorrow? It could be a death, divorce, career change. You would likely curl up in a ball and feel extreme pain, suffering and heartache.

That's not what we were meant to do on this earth when people leave our lives. We are meant to LOVE fully, be happy and experience JOY, even in the presence of sadness and grief.

The reality is that some of these things will happen in our lifetimes. But, no matter the grief, horrendous earth-shattering heartache and events that occur - we have the rest of our lives to live.

How we choose to move forward through grief with love, happiness and joy for ourselves is something I've found for myself, and I want to share with you.

> *If you are or were a victim of abuse as a child, teenager or adult, that trauma, those occurrences affect your relationships today and I encourage you to seek a therapist to help you along this journey.*

As we are here living in this beautiful body, why not seek JOY in our everyday interactions and life experiences?

YOU DESERVE TO LIVE EACH DAY TO ITS FULLEST!

Let's peel back the layers and be willing to be
BROKEN OPEN.

When the winds of change arise, you will have the seeds already planted within you, to recenter yourself over and over again, while continuously living on a higher vibration than you have ever lived before.

Chapter 7

YOU GOTTA HAVE FAITH TO BE CONNECTED

Being hopeful, positive and having faith is probably the most important and pronounced belief through your self- growth journey.

Beginning in 2018, my daughter experienced a health crisis and was subsequently diagnosed with a Primary Immune Deficiency Disease. During this stressful time in my life, one of the things I found helpful was to  create a website and blog to share my experiences with others. The act of blogging had a therapeutic effect.

Here is a passage from my blog, "Aubrey's Blog, From a Momma's Perspective" on AvasJourney.life

January 2, 2020 "You Gotta Have Faith"

We have entered into a new decade. What has happened for you over the past ten years? How is it that some days feel brutally long, yet the years have flown by in a blink!? Is your life now, what it was ten years ago? The same daily routine, the same people, parties, grind day in and day out. What does that look like? I imagine that would look and feel like you are stuck. As if you didn't evolve or grow. It would look kind of boring. The pressures of life that weighed on you ten years ago should no longer be.

What you have experienced in this past decade was GROWTH. We have new tasks, demands and stressors that we have walked through over the past 10 years. Even storms from a year ago have since brought sunshine to a new day. In the present, "preteen or tweenager" kinds of clouds that are currently brewing in my life. Those years that once seemed so far out of reach have suddenly smacked me right in the face. Like a brick wall that came out of nowhere and I slammed right into it.

Through my children, hardships, tough people, places and situations my spirituality has transformed into this amazing life altering space. It's hard to even put into words at times. I have experienced so much over the past decade. Things I once questioned and were hesitant to believe in- have paved paths, opened doors and guided me. When I hear people express their hesitation, question their beliefs- that they are not sure if they believe in God, the law of attraction or the universe I ask them why not.

Friends… I urge you to step back, take a breath and open up your heart and mind. Expect to be supported by the universe. Expect to have your prayers answered. Expect great things in your life. There is something much bigger than us that started all of this. Those "Aha!" moments, the miracles you witness or hear about; that's not luck. I don't believe in luck; I believe in FAITH.

Why do you ask? Because I am living proof. I am a catholic elementary school girl who questioned the system daily. The nuns and educators at my school weren't sure what to do with me. I didn't make it through the "Pledge of Allegiance" by 8:05am I was already being sent to the principal's office. I questioned EVERYTHING. I had my doubts- but then I had my son.

This was a miracle all on its own. The fact that my body could grow and nurture another human being. Pregnancy was the most incredible, miraculous experience of my life. And when that sweet baby boy was placed into my arms, EVERYTHING I thought I knew about life had cosmically changed. Life shifted and my relationship with God started for real. Having faith and truly believing in something bigger than myself. I started to actually ASK God/the universe, whatever you chose to call it, for things. We are all thinking, praying and speaking to the same higher divine being. Then watching my life unfold, come TRUE, though the shifts and doors that closed to only open bigger better ones is a remarkable experience. I know you have had this happen within your life. Many times, I presume. THAT is your faith. That is all you've asked for coming ahead- in divine time. TRUST GOD'S TIMING.

The knowing and believing that everything is going to work out. That you will have those things you've been asking and praying for- that new position at work, that beautiful house you desire, that relationship you long for- that breakthrough is on its way.   Trust God's timing. Let go of doubt, let go of your fears. Be vulnerable to the "idea" that something of a higher divine will always have your back. Because why not? Why not BELIEVE in something that feels so good? Something that is so positive and uplifting. What is the harm in having faith and believing in something or someone that is only speaking of positivity? Something we can give our children to lean on when they feel scared or alone. Teaching them they too are supported always by God and the universe.

Side note: I am not promoting any particular religion in this book. At this moment I am speaking of connecting to your spirituality, your soul-self. I believe all religions have it correct. I don't believe there is one right way. I do believe we are all speaking to a higher being.

Do you believe in the "magic" of Christmas? That feeling you get around the holidays that is uplifting and exciting? Do you believe or want to believe that when someone close to you is taken from this world too soon, that they go to heaven? Well, when holding my brand-new little baby boy, the universe expanded and I saw things clearer. It's like a veil had been lifted. I knew in that moment that heaven was for real and never doubted it since.

Because how could I ever imagine anything else now that I have been blessed with two children. When our loved ones die do you believe that's it - you go into a dark, black hole? Not a chance. Not for one second.

Connecting to my faith has made life itself easier.

If that sounds weird, it's not. It's my truth, it's light and fluffy and I LOVE this feeling. Do I have my doubts at times when a storm is in my path? Does fear creep in? Of course. But I recognize when that is happening and in a moment's notice, I choose love and I choose to lean into my soul-self and realign.

JOY became REAL and experienced through daily practice of having faith. Joy and fear cannot live in the same space at the same time. It's not possible. I choose joy daily. I choose to send love tunnels where there is fear and sadness. Just by saying the words "I choose" aloud is a GAME CHANGER. Try it. "I choose" is an affirmation that you and I have choices. No matter what is happening in your life, we 100% of the time ALWAYS have a choice.

It's become a daily practice and mantra for me. Just today my husband and I were having a disagreement about how to remodel our kitchen. Though we are very much in sync and on the same page, we have different opinions, views and ideas. The car ride was getting heated over picking our paint color for the kitchen cabinets. In the middle of the disagreement, out loud I said "I choose peace!" Those words shifted our entire conversation. It relaxed me, it relaxed him. I decided to honor our differences by sliding in a wildcard. We clearly weren't going to argue about a peace agreement.

"A New Year." That sentence can be very overwhelming. I welcome each new day as a blank canvas. I have faith that the prayers I laid out a year ago are still in manifestation mode. And I am willing to always have faith that yesterday's burdens won't follow me. Release the power anyone may have over your life.

Choose Joy. Choose to let go of the fear, move through love, and lean further into your faith. Start small.

Have faith that God, the universe, has your back. Put positive thoughts into motion. Heighten your daily vibration of living with love. Pour into love through everyone who walks in your path- through every hardship, dysfunction or storm you are put in. Not every single day will be sunshine, but on those stormy days, you get to choose what you want to be.

To view more blog posts,
visit www.AvasJourney.life
"Aubrey's Blog".

Chapter 8

SEPARATED VS KEPT

Being "separated" I define as being apart from ourselves.
Like puzzle pieces sitting in a box. All the pieces are there,
but not connected to create the image or final product. We
have all of the pieces inside of ourselves; *how* we learn to
identify where all the parts link together is an important
part of our journey.

When we are "kept" we are pieced together connecting
through the threads, corners and ridges that make us whole.
Once we are in a space of being
"kept," if a puzzle piece detaches or weakens, we are able
to sew that piece back to its place with ease.

Our soul-self lies inside of us - gives us guidance, like those gut feelings. How do we link the three - our mind, body and spirit - to stay in constant alignment at all times?

Through practice and guidance anything is possible.

When you discover this incredible soul-self power you hold, you reflect that like quality onto others. You become an example for others, which in turn, is serving humanity on a positive vibrational level.

Our soul lives inside of us and is clothed in our body, our human form. Our spirit is what leaves this earth when our hearts no longer beat inside our bodies. I believe our soul continues to live on and carries forth an even bigger purpose.

Do you believe that anything is possible?

I only speak about the paths that I have walked. My self-growth journey has not been an easy one. I have allowed myself to surrender my vulnerability, summoning strength, love and patience. Yet, the wisdom I have gained and continue to see, widens my lens more and more each day. My self-growth journey has been a positive life-changing shift for me and in turn for those around me.

You can do all things "self-care", like take a fishing trip, a mental health day, indulge at the spa, rest your eyes, or hop in a hot bubble bath. This is great stuff but here's the thing: If we don't know **who** we are and **what** we want - I mean what we *really* want - and don't align with both our soul-self and ego-self as one, that "self-care" will only be a temporary state of mind.

Why not choose to live in a space where you hold a *grounded center* controlled by you 100% of the time? Friends - there is so much more than what's on the surface. There is more to YOU. It's literally inside of you. Some of us just choose not to see or feel it, are fearful to lean inward, or ignore it and think it's not important.

YET, IT'S EVERYTHING!

Everything you've ever wanted to know, see and feel is held inside of YOU!

Let's stop worrying about the end of our life and start living in the present moments right in front of us.

We will journey on and continue to discover how to connect with our soul-self, know and learn to speak the truths of who we are from the inside out - *fully, wholly and authentically.*

It's time to stop living in fear and fall in love with the most important person in your life...YOU.

Chapter 9

YOU GET WHAT YOU GIVE

Everything I am speaking about comes down to the vibrational energy we give and receive to and from others, ourselves and the world as a whole. Every single thing is made up of energy. Our thoughts and feelings are sending and manifesting "like" thoughts and feelings to return to us.

Think about that for a second. I strongly believe that good and bad energy within an individual, cannot exist at the same time in the same space. Recognize that *you* have the power to be in control of your thoughts.

By choosing to think positively you will shape your karma and Universal Law of Attraction. It's kind of like the sayings, "treat others how you want to be treated" and "whatever we think and do to others, we will eventually experience ourselves."

The Law of Attraction is believed by many to be the universal law of "like attracts like." There have been many books written on the Law of Attraction. Like a magnet, we attract our "like" match.

To put it simply - if you think or act in negative thoughts and behaviors, you're attracting negative thoughts/behaviors to come back to you. If you think or act in positive thoughts/behaviors, you will have that 'like' positive attraction.

As you move through this journey, I highly recommend reading or listening to books on audible like *The Energy Bus* and *The Secret.* If you read them before, read them again. Things speak differently a second, third or even tenth time around.

Now that you have begun this self-growth journey, grey areas that you once overlooked will start to jump out at you; objects will begin to look clearer and sharper. The kind of things that you weren't ready to observe before you'll find yourself embracing.

I've been on this journey - my self-growth journey - for almost a decade now and I am dedicated to continuing my practice to evolve even more.

I am not the same person I was 5 years ago, 10 years ago or even yesterday. And I hope to be a better version of myself tomorrow than I am today.

When you make the choice to practice and heighten your positive vibrational frequencies - like thoughts, feelings,

actions - you level up! You have the capability to continue to evolve into the next-best version of yourself, in small doses.

This personal self-growth journey is not a "quick-fix."

Life-shifts don't happen overnight and they take patience, practice, discipline and work.

Very few of us are disciplined enough to jump in with both feet and get started. Most of us may need guidance like a life coach, therapist, self-growth opportunities or an accountability partner for our own growth and expansion. It takes effort and work.   If you want to always be growing and find that sweet spot; do things in love. ALL THINGS. Even the people and places we do not favor. Think and act of them in love.

I have never been one to follow the crowd. Ballet gave me a strong discipline and confidence at a young age. It helped to mold me into who I am today.

There was a movement that was big on Social Media in 2019: "Evolve OR Repeat." It struck me as a limiting or constraining concept; I saw it differently.

I adopted the philosophy: **EVOLVE & Repeat >>**

What does this mean? It means, once I learn methods to evolve and propel myself forward in the direction I desire most, I then repeat the process that got me there. Apply this philosophy to _all_ areas in your life: continually EVOLVING & Repeating>>.

MAKE SENSE?

I started a YouTube Channel in 2019 called **Aubrey Conley Intuitive Power Life Coach : EVOLVE & Repeat>>**. I felt called to speak my truths and give people topics to think about, engage for all to feel safe and welcomed; giving others the opportunities to _give themselves permission_ to see their own growth in hearing my tales.

Interestingly enough many questioned my title and how it made sense, since some saw it as a negative phrase. I LOVE when things speak to everyone differently and it creates a conversation for expansion, wisdom and growth.

The paths I traveled on my self-growth journey caused my eyes to open widely and my heart to see and speak things very differently than once before.

(You will learn more about the details in my own journey in my next book 😆).

My self-growth journey kept widening my eyes.

> _I saw people and places with a heightened sense of awareness and I felt space continuously opening up inside of me. At the time I was not fully understanding the shifts, changes and transitions that my frequency levels and my "vibes" were reaching._
>
> _I never saw myself as average. I was always aware that I had a unique eye for things, especially in the art of dance. Being a choreographer, dance teacher and_

mentor, I could envision movements and performances in every detail before the choreography was even written. I've always had the ability to pick apart tiny things, almost hidden to the naked eye.

In addition, I feel that I have an empathetic connection with children; the ability to sense a need or vulnerability.

I know each person is unique and no two kids should be treated exactly the same, because they are not the same.

I always knew I was great at what I did for a living because of this insight.   The wiser I grew, I learned this unique quality I held inside of me went way beyond just my career and rings true throughout every single aspect of my life. No one taught me this power, this inward connection. This is something I put extreme effort, love and attention to finding for myself.

Each day presents a new opportunity to EVOLVE.

Choose to "**EVOLVE**" and strive to "**REPEAT>>**" the process: "level-up" - maximizing your growth and reaching your highest potential for that day. "Keep Calm & Carry On."

On your journey, there could be a point where you feel completely satisfied or settled, as if you climbed the highest mountain and are holding an award because of it. Congratulations! Celebrate! Pat yourself on the back. You've added a piece to your puzzle. Now...keep going!

Your self-growth journey will be an ever-present, ongoing, never-ending trip that will continue throughout your lifetime.

At times, you may find yourself stuck. Recognize you've plateaued and there is a need to keep practicing. Go back into your toolbox and utilize the resources you've used to get you this far.

Don't allow this "stuck feeling" to keep you from your "already, always-knowing."

Get out of your own way and find a seed that you had previously planted; something that brings you LOVE or JOY.

When you feel blocked is when a new door is ready to be opened, to obtain more growth and wisdom!

Water that seed and start again.

Once you have connected with your soul-self you will be able to continue to *level-up*, seeing things with amazing focus: ideas, feelings, creativities and energies become magnified.

I believe that when we experience this awakening, our energies will naturally pour onto others as an example of how to grow within themselves, too. Consequently, our positive vibes will flow to our family, friends and most importantly to the youth with whom we interact in our daily lives.

Choose to honor the growth inside of you and foresee how it will benefit those closest to you. Connecting with one's soul-self, at any age, will break the chains that hold us back from living freely from our core.

Start by sharing this book with your village.

Imagine the confidence and self-love we could instill by sharing this discovery with the people in our lives.

How great would it be to witness those people who surround us begin to build a positive, loving relationship with themselves?! So many hardships and internal struggles could be avoided if one knew how to make friends and love themselves. This is how we continue the spread of kindness and show love for one another around the world.

If I could go back and tell my younger self what I know now: that I have to fully accept and love myself before I can truly love and positively take care of and impact others. To appreciate myself. To create a positive relationship with my body - both inside and out. To be my own best friend. I would have created the connection with my soul-self a lot sooner in life. But I truly trust everything and every moment has happened for a reason and it has led me to where I am today. Each day I choose to live my life to its fullest.

When your soul-self is available "on demand" then whatever is happening around you won't affect your full state of being, *unless* you allow it to.

Recognizing those moments and reaching inside to empower yourself may be one of the hardest things you've ever done. But the benefits you reap once connected to your soul-self will be the most rewarding you will ever experience in your life.

You will fall multiple times and it can take years before aligning with your soul-self becomes second nature. But the most important schooling you will ever do as a human and spiritual being is to think, speak and act purposefully.

Practice the pause... and rely on your centered soul-self to make the choices that will affect your entire being and those who feel your vibrations.

Do you want to live and be fully open to receive insight and opportunities?

Do you want to be really fulfilled and aligned with the universe?

YES!

Congratulations!

By saying 'YES!'

You have just begun.

Chapter 10

⇥ *ME* ⇤

There is so much work to do on your personal soul-self journey. It all starts with the word ⇥**ME**⇤.

What do you see when you separate the letters **M** and **E**?

The "**M**" stands for ME (you) and the "**E**" stands for EVERYONE ELSE.

We must take care of ourselves, fill up _our_ buckets first - nourish and replenish ourselves in order to fully, presently and authentically pour our love and joy onto others.

So, in this chapter we are focusing on the ⇥ **M** ⇤ = **ME (you).**

> *My all-time favorite children's book is "Have You Filled a Bucket Today?" by Carol McCloud. This book tells a story about how we all carry an imaginary bucket. By saying and doing nice things for others fills up their buckets and ours, too. A great read for any adult. It will illuminate and widen your perspective on this new journey you've stepped into.*

It's important to have yourself "filled up"- like a tall glass of water - filled to capacity. Once you fill it to the top, don't stop there! Continue pouring into that glass as you are now able to *overflow* with love and gratitude onto others.

When this happens you continuously peak to a high vibration, keeping yourself filled with love, joy and clarity like never before.

There is a saying: how do you look at your cup - half empty or half full?

My answer to that is I'm happy to ***have*** a cup!

Finding GRATITUDE in your soul-self journey is very important.

Maintaining your "true north" is a pivotal part of your own journey.

There are two important things that you should leave behind as you continue to embark on this journey:
1. Excuses (Playing Victim)
2. Laziness

If you constantly have a "reason or excuse" for why or how something happened to you, you will never have the opportunity to expand your mind, look inward and see how that circumstance is holding you back due to your thoughts.

No one is coming to save you. You have to put your newly found positive thoughts into action.

You are reading this book and on this personal self-growth journey, expansion and discovery to create a stronger, safer, excellent relationship with YOU.

If you want a better life, more opportunities, a better job, a bigger home, more money, a perfect partner, a kinder teenager, there are three major commitments that need to be made: And remember: the sky's the limit!

1. Find your soul-self: practice every day to seek that space.
2. Stop making excuses for yourself and others - victimizing, falling into lazy patterns that don't serve you and those around you who are feeling your energy.
3. Start by doing something about it. Recognize your thoughts, words and actions. Be mindful.

This is an "in-your-face" realization.

If you're offended by this, you probably need to look deeper into the mirror. Think about your habits, your social media posts, your thoughts, whispers and reactions to other people's lives.

We all have a few dozen excuses as to why we are where we are. But we have the control to gracefully take back our power and get connected with our soul-self. If you choose to be willing to put in the efforts and want to be better - you *will* be.

Limiting Beliefs / Mindset Reset Positive Affirmation
I always end up here
I've already tried everything
I don't have time
I don't know how
It's my parents' fault
I don't have the money
The weather is affecting me
I was raised this way
This is who I am
I'm too old
I can't afford it
I have no luck

Do you see all of those excuses?

That's ⇸ **ME** ↤ not fulfilled.

The ⇸ **ME** ↤ is thinking and believing its fears. These are highly negative vibrational thoughts and words you have put into the universe. Others are feeling your vibe, and like I've been saying this whole time, "you get what you give." You are attracting exactly what you don't want by thinking and speaking about what you *don't* want.

Be a reflection of what you desire, it's that simple. There is no need to overthink this process. Once you start thinking about yourself, make a friendship with yourself and impact your own life in a positive way; you can open a window of opportunity to make a friend with you.

BE IN LOVE WITH YOU

These small steps are pieces to assist you in figuring out who you are and will lead you to your soul-self, where you are able to manifest your future, control your emotions and reactions, and hold power in your life.

Resetting your mindset matters!

- You need to save you.
- You need to WANT to save yourself.

We have such a short time on this planet and the fact that you woke up today and have the opportunity to read this book is enough purpose to start again.

You have to fill the ⟶ **M** ⟵ with LOVE in order to share your love with everyone else ⟶ **E** ⟵.
Grab a pen. Here's your first assignment.

First, ask yourself what do you want?

Write down as many things that come to your mind.

For example: *I want financial freedom.*
              I want a housekeeper. I want to be whole.

| |
| |
| |
| |
| |

Second, WHO ARE YOU? Who do you want to be? And if you don't know, it's time to start focusing on who the heck you really are.

> NOTE: _not_ defined by the world, or as others see you: mom, wife, nurse, lawyer - but as _you_ see yourself - how you think about yourself, for example: "I am positive; I am powerful; I am beautiful; I sing beautifully; I make a difference in the world".

My name is:
I am:

Finally, see the list of limiting beliefs in the beginning of this chapter? Any that apply to you, write a positive affirmation changing the thought and recognizing the keys to resetting _your mindset_.

For example:
I can't afford it = I can afford it.

As soon as you say _"I can't"_ not only are you putting that negative vibration into the world to come back to you, but your thoughts manifest into your beliefs and become your reality.

What if you began to prioritize some life goals?

When we are clear about what we want to ourselves and to the universe - that empowerment places "high vibe thoughts" into motion, clearly and more quickly.

The universe will in return send you messages reinforcing that you are on the path of attracting that "like" vibration. You just need to be willing to see things from a different view.

You get to choose to be the architect of your life!

You CAN make time for the things in life that are important to you, while still being intentional to yourself and your family. Give yourself permission to think, speak and act on purpose.

I wish you could take a peek inward and see what it's like to be in this powerful space, inside your soul-self. I have so much faith in you; have faith in yourself and grant yourself permission to jump in with both feet. Jump into the swimming pool of your personal self-growth journey by finding the truest love and friendship of all: that which you have with yourself.

This powerful personal inward space you hold within you, is untouchable from others. No one else can touch or see your soul-self. It's there for only you to count on and lean into. Choosing to make excuses, having a fixed mindset, putting terms and conditions on things and people - put all that aside!

To continuously open more space and choose to step into those positive moments that show up - recognize and believe there are <u>no</u> limits! You get to start over and over again in any moment.

Knowing and trusting you are *never* truly alone is something I WISH for you.

WHY? you may ask.

Why do I wish for my family and friends to live at the highest vibration of purity and love? Why do I wish for <u>all</u> to recognize, feel and have the ability to tap into this powerful vibrational space I've found within myself?

WHY do I want this for each person ?

They could be strangers: those I may pass in the grocery store or drive behind in traffic, bump into accidentally in the coffee shop and those across the world in other countries.

EVEN those who are no longer in my life because of broken ties or turned paths... I genuinely want them all to live in love, joy and happiness in their daily lives.

I purposefully choose to send a love tunnel, each and every day, to others - with pure intentions of JOY, LOVE and HAPPINESS - 'as wide as an ocean' - for their highest good - - in hopes they feel pulled to submerge their entire self into finding this space inside of them.

This is what I've been called to do in my journey and I have accepted the invitation and stepped into my authentic-self: sharing, spreading and impacting through this level of high vibrational love for <u>ALL of humanity</u>. Because that is who I am. I have chosen to <u>purposefully</u> take responsibility in my life for my thoughts, feelings, spoken and unspoken words and actions. This is the energy I choose to put into the universe and the energy I want to attract back to me.

There is no room in this powerful soul-self space for resentment, worry and fear - it no longer exists and it's so FREEING!!

I encourage you to get started with one thing, person or place in your life that is uncomfortable. Meaning: turning INWARD, looking at your reflection. That 'one thing' opens space inside of you for 2, 3, 4 more things - and the association of your *own* true self-awareness will light up with each transitional step you take.

This doesn't mean relationships will mend or be fixed; that's not the point at all! This is for YOU, your well-being, health, happiness and authentic self.

Remember **you** picked up this book and have already come thus far, don't quit now. You are here with me, in this moment for a reason - an exploration, curiosity or maybe for a change. So, let's get rid of those limiting beliefs you're holding onto.

You are never too old and it is never too late.

Chapter 11
SURRENDER

"When we surrender our will to the power of the universe, we receive miracles."
- The Universe Has Your Back, Gabrielle Bernstein

To consciously build a strong support for ourselves, brick by brick, we must first surrender the things that don't serve us.

> Surrender having to be in control.
> Surrender being out of control.
> Surrender any fear and worry.
> Surrender the what-ifs.

Make the choice of what comes next in your life. You truly hold the power to turn the tide. Those gut urges, the knee-jerk reactions: guilt, envy, jealousy, self-doubt, worry, and excuses - recognize you have them, then let them go.

Give it up to the heavens to handle for you. You're not required to carry any negative weight.

> *I believe we are children of God and his angels are right next to us, yes right next to YOU, in this very second and ready to take on your burdens and troubles.*

Life is not about keeping up with the Joneses, whose schedules are busier, pleasing your in-laws, or living up to the expectations of others.

Life is about LOVE, finding your JOY, who YOU are. Doing the things you want to do and when you want to do them - flying high like an arrow at full speed, forward; into the next moment. While staying open to receiving and giving more love and joy.

I consider connecting a friendship within ourselves as an opportunity to give ourselves permission. Permission to love harder and feel deeper.

Our own senses are heightened beyond our imagination to hearing and seeing things more clearly, and our intuition strengthens. Walls that once felt unbreakable crumble, your breathing deepens and you become aware of the energy within your own cells.

> *I am more connected with the cells inside my own body than ever before. I wish I was this deeply connected when I was pregnant with my children. I can only imagine the feelings and communication I would have been able to have had with them in my womb!*

You owe it to yourself, to connect with your soul-self, the rest will fall into place from there. It's pretty incredible how the
colors of my life have brightened, deepened and even have a sharpened edge to them than ever before. I no longer stress or hold resentments of the past and am not anxious about the future.

It's like putting on glasses for the first time without even realizing that things were not clear to your vision before.

I choose to live in the present moments - <u>my presence</u> – where and who I am with in the moment.

Surrender having to be in control.

Surrender being out of control.

Surrender any fear and worry.

Surrender the 'what-ifs'.

Surrender yourself to awareness; a perspective-shifting experience - a true awakening space to live.

Chapter 12

FORGIVENESS

Forgiveness is the foundation of our personal self-growth journey. Each of us has had times where we have done or said things that were not our best moments; and there has been hurt put upon us by others.

ARE YOU STILL LIVING THERE?

Are you circling around and around in your head, thinking back to a situation or conversation wondering how it could have been different? Or why someone did what they did or said what they said to you?

There is so much opportunity waiting to be awakened within our hearts if we could move beyond old emotional hurt. By focusing inward - using the energy of LOVE, to look at past relationships and disagreements - we can begin to repair those spaces in our hearts where we once failed to forgive.

In order to fully love yourself, it's important to release resentment, anger, hurt, confusion, judgement and any feelings of being <u>stuck</u> that are held inside of you.   It's time to have closure, to forgive *yourself and others* in order for <u>you</u> to move forward.

You may not even realize it but this affects your choices, judgments and other relationships throughout your life.

Choose to release the power a person or situation may have over you. By choosing to hold on to any anger or resentment of the past - I can promise you, you're not hurting the person who hurt you, you're only hurting yourself with the negative energy you're stuck in.

Forgive those who have done you wrong.

We all come from different backgrounds and each of us deserve to experience a life of JOY. It's time to GROW. It's time to let go of your shortcomings, any self-doubt, and anything or anyone who is holding you back from having full freedom to experience the pure joy hidden inside of you.

Grab a pen, a fresh sheet of paper and get ready to write the toughest letter of your life. This next exercise is a building-block towards the path of discovering your soul-self. This practice will bless you with the breakthrough you need to move forward.

Don't skip this exercise, friends!

This is a HUGE part of *growing* through what you've *gone* through and **connecting** to your soul-self.

In order to prevail and renew, we have to dig through the trenches of mud inside ourselves, and be willing to acknowledge our 'stuff' - any triggers and bad habits that hold us down. We need to recognize them in order to move onward and know what we <u>don't want</u>. Don't worry - you will not mail this letter.

Forgiveness is for you, not for them. Forgiveness releases the power that person or thing holds over you and will also release the emotional attachment you may have with them from your life.

Whoever you are, wherever you are, the choice is yours. We can choose to be *right* and set in our own ways or we can choose to *repair* those places inside us.

Write your 'forgiveness letter':
- ❑ *release the power that a person or situation may have over you*
- ❑ *bring into full focus the first trigger, person or situation that comes to mind*
- ❑ *close your eyes and feel the emotions that come up and allow them to surface.*

Write today's date and begin your letter with

Dear _____,

There are three important parts to your letter.

1. Start your first sentence with "I forgive you for what you did to me," and let your pen continue writing from there. Be specific, even if it hurts or is painful to relive.

2. Show Gratitude for what they brought into your life. No matter what happened something came out of that relationship
    before, during or after that hurt. A lesson, a direction, a person; think about it and acknowledge it.

3. Your final paragraph should focus on the Silver-lining YOU discovered through this exercise.

I promise your pen will hit the paper and will take off.
The hardest part is getting started.
Choose to not hold anything back and get all the thoughts, emotion and feelings out of your head.

Once you complete and sign your letter, fold the letter into squares or place into a sealed envelope.

Now you are ready for the next step: RELEASING

I've found the physical act of writing my forgiveness letter is extremely beneficial to my internal healing and cleans out old wounds opening space to expand my inner soul-self connection.   What I choose to do with it next is even more exhilarating.

I take that letter and light it up immediately!

I toss it in my fireplace and watch it burn; or I take my letter over to the sink and light it on fire.

As I watch my letter turn to ash, the weight of hurt, anger, resentment and any fears literally peel away, and those heavy corners that were once in my heart feel lightened.

Here's an alternative to turning your letter to ash.

In our home we have another method I created called the "Triangle of Trust."

My Triangle of Trust

When someone has worries or needs to "give it up to God," we put our letter or message in the "Triangle of Trust."

A mix of crystals, stones, sometimes even seashells, (all which hold energy) are placed in a triangular shape on a table in our home.

When someone is concerned with worries or fears that are holding them back from their joy; we place our letter, note or word right in the middle of the triangle.

Sometimes, my children find healing by merely placing their letter in the "Triangle of Trust" without the extra step of burning it. That act alone leaves them feeling free of that burden.

You may have written a forgiveness letter but are not quite ready to release or forgive this person fully. Putting your letter in a book or a "Triangle of Trust" may be enough for you at that moment.

The purpose of this exercise is to **fully release** and let go of that burden you bare. If you feel the need to write more letters, do it! Get that negative energy out. The more you release the more room you create for love to flow.

Continue practicing this exercise to propel you into the next step on your self-growth journey of finding your soul-self.

You deserve to take back your power and open up more space inside your heart for new happiness and deeper love.

If you need more guidance or understanding of this exercise, please tune in to my YouTube channel Aubrey Conley : INTUITIVE POWER LIFE COACH >>EVOLVE & Repeat>> Forgiveness Episode 6.

Chapter 13
TURN THE TIDE

On my journey to find my soul-self, I came upon an inspirational speaker and author, Esther Hicks. She speaks often about the Law of Attraction and the Universal Flow of Life.

Basically, Hicks says that life is like a stream that flows. We can choose to resist it and swim against the current or we can choose to go in the stream's direction with ease.

Either way it still flows.

Would you prefer to always be fighting against the current of life? Swimming upstream is an emotionally and physically exhausting way to live.

> *No, thank you. I consciously recognize these occurrences and make the decision to choose again.*

If you *expect* your life to always be great it <u>will</u> be.

> A *self-fulfilling prophecy* is the socio-psychological phenomenon of someone "predicting" or expecting something, and this "prediction" or expectation coming true simply because the person believes it will and the person's resulting behaviors align to fulfill the belief. This suggests that people's beliefs influence their actions.

The Law of Attraction is always in your favor.

It's easy to say *turn your fears into love*, but how do you do that?

We can make a conscious choice to remain on a frequency of LOVE no matter what drops in our path. The news, a negative coworker, the morning off to a rough start, a flat tire; whatever the excuse. Because that's what it is...an excuse to feel negative - recognize this!

Reset your mindset, recognizing that the thoughts you choose will repeatedly go-round-and-round in your mind, becoming a self-fulfilling prophecy.

Make sure those thoughts are *positive* ones about yourself, others and the world.

It doesn't mean you can't question things or listen to opinions. Gaining information and educating yourself on a topic, person or difference of opinion is part of the journey; it's important to get all your facts from a 360-degree view because this will help shape your future self.

Do we automatically wake up joyful every day? No way! There are ways to change our mindset, to *turn the tide* and move things into a more positive direction. Working toward this "change in mindset" all begins with YOU and YOUR ideal alignment with your soul-self.

Think of this as a "voyage of self- discovery".

This process will take some time - months, even years - to connect, and this path is never-ending - <u>always growing</u>. It's important to hear me when I say that…
"ALWAYS GROWING."

Your momentum of growth will depend on how open you are to the idea of self-alignment and surrendering your fixed mindsets and narrowed ways you choose to view yourself, others and the world.

To keep this momentum growing will require practice to keep you connected and help propel you forward.

We have adapted to ignoring our soul-self for so long, not even realizing it is a part of us because of outside influence and life's distractions: negative social media, malls filled with "stuff," viewing other people's lives, casting negative judgements and being judged. These things pull us further away from our own "already, always-knowing" inner guidance.

Your soul-self, that connection you're searching for - it's right there inside of you! Though we can't see it or touch it, we can feel it.

In order to *autocorrect* back to the center of ourselves - *choosing* to think and move through **positive** daily habits - it takes *practice* and getting comfortable with being uncomfortable in moments. There will be things that may make you uncomfortable.

This is another important growth lesson: *get comfortable with being uncomfortable.* This is a necessary part of your journey for growth to take place.

Let's begin with a daily mindful practice.

Meditation.

Chapter 14

MINDFULNESS THROUGH MEDITATION

If you are not familiar with meditation, download an app or watch a YouTube video to get an idea of how it works.

Through my husband's and my own experiences (initially my husband would never have entertained this idea) we have found that meditation is the **bridge** between *you* and the **connection** to *your soul-self.*

Meditation is an important tool that we use to tune into our physical being, connecting with our spiritual being; by honoring our inner power and choosing to live in each moment through love.

Just start, even if you're not sure what you are doing. Daily meditation is a must to fully align with your soul-self.

Keep a notebook near you during this time. You can meditate anywhere at any time of the day. By passing up a 10–15-minute window to recenter yourself and learn more about **you** is a truly missed personal growth opportunity.

In the warmer months, I like to meditate outside in nature, sitting in the grass or by the ocean. I meditate in my bedroom before my family awakens in the morning, prior to my yoga practice, and sometimes in my car when I arrive at a place and have a few extra moments to myself (instead of scrolling social media or checking email.)

Here is an easy focus meditation I created for myself and share with you.

EVOLVE & Repeat>> 10-Minute Focus Meditation Exercise:

I recommend putting on some meditation or soft piano music in the background, then setting a timer.

Don't forget your notebook and pen!

Owl Artwork By: Efthimia Cardwell

Step 1.

Start by sitting in a seated position on the floor, outside in nature or in your car.

Be sure to hold good posture with your neck long, ears aligned with your shoulders - shoulders back - heart feeling open and palms face-up or down, resting on your knees.

> *My husband finds his meditation works best lying flat on a yoga mat on his back.*

Step 2.

Close your eyes and think about those seven chakras for a moment.

Envision that straight line throughout your body.

> *If you use essential oils, I invite you to use them as you meditate. Essential oils raise frequency levels and heighten the experience. Place the oil of choice in your hands and slowly breathe them in prior to starting, a drop on your crown and on your heart.*

Step 3.

Begin to breathe in slowly through your nose for 5 seconds.

Exhale through your nose or mouth (whatever feels natural to you) for 5 seconds.

Repeat for a full minute.

Then...

Begin to slowly extend your breath to an 8-second inhale and an 8-second exhale. Think about moving from the belly, to the lungs, then chest - in that order, as you inhale and exhale.

Repeat for a minute.

Fill up your lungs fully and then release to empty out your breath completely.

Once you've gotten into a breathing flow; recognize where your thoughts wander and shift your focus back onto listening to your breathing.

The goal is to focus on listening to your own breath.

Step 4.

Breathe deeply in an 8-second inhale, now PAUSE.

(Holding that inhaled breath for 4 seconds of stillness)

Exhale for 8 seconds completely, emptying your lungs, now PAUSE again, holding for 4 seconds of stillness.)

- *I find that the pauses to find space between the inhale and exhale are so valuable in this journey.*

Repeat this breathing pattern for the rest of your meditation.

I've found it helpful to begin my practice by setting an intention. Something as simple as inviting in 'love' for myself. Inhale love and exhale love. Allowing myself to receive love and send love out into the universe. Into nature, all people and all living things all over the world. Always coming back to that breath.

Step 5. Once your timer has gone off, continue to breathe but affirm out loud and inward "I am love, I give love, I receive love, I spread love to all."

I like to repeat this affirmation several times and If a mirror is in front of me, I choose to look at myself by looking into my eyes deeply, with love... This is all about connecting with the ↦ **M** ↤

Step 6. Once your meditation is complete, grab a pen and write down in your notebook how you feel.

Did your vibes rise?

Did your energy shift?

 I keep a notebook in my purse, in my car, at my desk and by my bedside. When you get a thought, always write it down and date it.

This is a GREAT practice to do before entering into work, an appointment, picking up your kids from school.   An opportunity to reset your mindset and carve out a little space for yourself.

Give yourself some appreciation, you're on your way!

Chapter15

BLURRED LINES

This particular chapter is jam-packed with a lot of "food for thought." It might feel like you are on a merry-go-round as we'll revisit some of the concepts we talked about in earlier chapters. I encourage you to read this chapter several times to absorb the message.

If you want the ability of stepping into your soul-self to become second nature, then you must practice the techniques I'm sharing with you.

Remember, things don't happen overnight. It takes practice and patience to achieve progress.

On my quest for my soul-self journey I came across the book THE SECRET by Rhonda Byrne. I found many helpful concepts in her book that I applied on my journey.

In her book, she speaks about the *Law of Attraction* and describes the word *LOVE:*

> *"The feeling of love is the highest frequency you can emit. The greater the love you feel and emit, the greater the power you are harnessing."*
>
> — Rhonda Byrne

So, when I use the word LOVE I am describing what I identify as *my* highest vibrational frequency.

Rhonda also says, "that attaining this LOVE frequency is necessary in order for us to feel and reach for our "like" attraction."

When you change your mind set on the topic, you change your outcome .

Think of a specific "thing" you want in life that you currently don't have.

It can be anything from materialistic to emotional.

Write it down.

Some examples are, to:

Be successful in your career.
Buy a new car.
Want a new home.
Go on a vacation.
Want more money.
Have a life partner.
Fall in love.
Open a coffee shop.

Start a side hustle.
Be fulfilled- happy.
Remodel your kitchen.
Less anxiety and more focus.
Buy a vacation home.
Be content.

So how do you change *your thoughts* to get what you want?

In order to attract that "like match" - person, place or thing that we want - we need to be thinking and reaching for the highest vibrational thought that puts us at a frequency for the universe to attract that "like" match.

I spent years struggling to scale my business to grow to be profitable. Owning a dance studio is a true labor of love and I didn't get into the industry to be a millionaire - but at the end of the day, ME as the business owner who put everything I had into starting and building this place, making it beautiful and inviting for children and families - I was financially taking far less of a paycheck, "if any at all." This not only became a financial struggle for my personal household but an emotional struggle on my self-growth and impacted my daily life.

I needed to change my mindset on money in order to attract what I wanted - which was financial freedom and the ability to grow my business financially so families and children were able to continue to receive the positive impact my dance studio made throughout our community and others journey's.

I began taking online classes, studying the Zig Ziglar, Rachel Hollis and Suzy Ormans of the world and they along with many others had a strong impactful bottom line message: I needed to change my relationship with money, change my vibrational attraction to money - choose to love and appreciate money and it would love and appreciate me back.

I don't choose to love money over people or over my morals and values. I choose to love money to support my independence and success of living my life in its full fruition, able to serve humanity and give back to others all over the world.

So...let's talk about money.

Rhonda Byrne says:

"The only reason any person does not have enough money is because they are blocking money from coming to them with their thoughts."

I want to give YOU some food for thought about how you may relate with money.

You are struggling to pay your bills and you frantically want more money. But every time you think about money, you think about *not* having enough and *no way* to make more. Each time you think about wishing you **had** more and *not* having enough, you are sending a *negative* vibration of *not* having enough into the universe. Therefore, the universe is going to give you the vibration you put out: "*not* enough."

You GET what you GIVE - make sense?

When the negative feeling of *not having enough* comes into thought, send it a love tunnel; feel **love** and appreciation for money in your heart and live in that space.

"I love money, money loves me" has been a practice and repeated saying from Rhonda Byrne's book *"The Secret"* as well as MANY other financial gurus all over the world.

Repeat it over and over all day, every day.

Make post-it notes, write it in a journal, whatever it takes to turn your conversation ->your relationship <- with money into a positive one.

Have faith that if you love something on a positive level, **it** will love you back. (No matter what it is).   Over and over send a love tunnel coming from your heart directly to, in this case, money. You are training your subconscious to be receptive, to approach money in a positive way.

Appreciate money. Keep it gently in your wallet, not crumbled up in your pocket.   How you treat it is how you will attract it.

Just like everything else in life!!

Before you know it, money will start showing up - as subtle as pennies found on the ground.

Appreciate these signs, even if it is just pennies found on the ground. Say out loud, acknowledging for yourself and the universe, the shift in your energy and your new mindset with money.

When suddenly things begin to "show up" - in the means you ask for because you changed your thought process - it's because you choose to be clear to yourself and the universe about what you wanted...

This is referred to as "driftwood" - a metaphor for the universe's way of showing you that it's responding to what you're asking for.

If the topic of money causes you to have thoughts of fear or worry, recognize that you are putting that like attraction out there and shut it down. Do jumping jacks right there on the spot, skip, dance or sing; put on a song you love and turn up the volume. Do something to *shift* your mindset and remove that negative thought.

So, let's take that same way of thinking when it comes to **LOVE**.

You're lonely, and long for a life partner. Maybe you want to fall in love either with your current partner or are searching for one.

Choose to turn that dark feeling to light.
When you see people "in love," embrace it; gravitate towards that feeling of love.

Smile, be happy for other people thriving, and acknowledge the existence of that relationship.

Imagine what it would feel like to have something like that in your life.

If the thought of **never** having love occurs, or you feel resentment, jealousy or sadness that you don't have what others do - you are limiting the path to receive love.

Recognize that you are feeding your thought of love with a negative take on love!   Embrace and feel joy for your friend from work whose Facebook post was about her and her partner renewing their vows. *Live* in that heightened space of happiness for them as a celebration within yourself. Be genuinely happy for others in love, in life and YOU will attract that "like" feeling of love to yourself.

Empathy and compassion are a huge part of your self-growth journey.

Make sense? What can you do?

Remember that time you set a goal and nailed it? How proud and satisfied did you feel? Bought that car, paid off that loan. Are you still full of that exact enthusiasm and satisfaction today from that past mountain climb or goal met?

The idea is to continuously live *every day* in that feeling of success and happiness while moving onward into the next day, the next "climb in life." When we keep our energy positive and frequency high, we, one: reflect that light onto others as a ray of sunshine; and, two: we attract more of that "sunshine" - that positive energy.

Not everyone reading this book will put in the work to connect with their soul-self and begin their self-growth journey.

That's okay.

> You have to _be_ willing, committed and ready
>   to want more
>   for yourself
>   for your life
>   for those counting on you.

You have a choice to carry on with life as it is, or you can choose to open up and meet **yourself** to the fullest degree and live the way you really want to: EVERY. SINGLE. DAY.

I choose JOY.

Chapter 16

CALMING THE CRAZY

I am once again reminding you getting started is the hardest part and none of this is easy, but it's positively life shifting and transformational.

Let's say you want to work on this- find your '*soul-self*' - work on building a friendship with yourself - but the realities of your day-to-day life seem to leave little time for a "personal self-growth journey."

> Full-time job
> Dishes to wash,
> laundry to fold,
> Kids to feed
> Work to get done
> Groceries to buy
> Appointments to make...
> Lots of "STUFF" - am I right?

We all have similar types of obligations.

You have a choice: try to do it all and feel overwhelmed; or, you can take a deep breath, and take your time to decide what is the most important task.

Ask yourself: how can I begin to center my soul-self if I am *manically* trying to do everything? And what is the long term GAIN if I make space in my own daily life to do this thing now?

> *Something I find helpful is to create a physical list - maybe keep paper by my bed - so I can jot it down and get it off of my mind, knowing it won't be forgotten.*
>
> *An excellent resource journal I recommend is The High-Performance Planner by Brendon Burchard. Grab one. It will help you compartmentalize, find gratitude and plan day-by-day with EASE.*

Remember, if you are constantly giving yourself a ride on the merry-go-round - in the same "stuck" place - there is a lesson to be learned. The same concept may apply to your *relationships:* on a "merry-go-round" - attracting the same negativity. Maybe you think everyone else is the problem. Well - time to lean into that self-awareness mode a little more.

Lean into the uncomfortable idea that *you* are your own stumbling block, and work on it.

So, the next time you feel yourself stuck in cement or chaos has taken over you'll be able to walk away from that situation knowing you're self-assured and on a different vibration than you were before. Take a look around you. Your home, your car, your bedroom. How you live is how you feel inside. Be mindful of ALL the areas in your life- they go hand and hand.

When this happens, you WILL FEEL something inside of you SHIFT; then BOOM! you learned a lesson - you just had ***GROWTH***.

Tips and Tricks to Use When You're Feeling Stuck:
1. Meditate
2.Take an Epsom salt bath.
3. Get outside and go for a walk.

Watch the world around you move, the animals, trees; feel the wind at your back. Make a connection with the tiniest creatures mother nature nurtures.
4. Write. Keep a journal and write about your feelings.
Write "I AM LOVE, I AM PROTECTED, I AM JOY."

Get your feelings out- all of them, even the negative ones out of the space in your head and onto the page. A lift will occur by doing this practice regularly. Use the "Triangle of Trust" exercise.

Think about looking at your life through a blurry lens - if you could change the lens - you'd see clearer. Your vision becomes 20/20.

Instead of squinting through the fog
CHOOSE TO CHANGE THE LENS

This naturally happens when you find that connection to your soul-self and are fully aligned when _who you are_ and _who you want to be_ are in agreement with one another.

OKAY - this all _sounds_ great, but _how_ do I go about it?

You would _think_ knowing yourself would be easy. Unfortunately, for the majority of us, it's probably the most difficult relationship to seek out and the hardest person to make friends with.

We are used to taking care of everyone else before ourselves. Self-love is not just self-care and as we learned in prior chapters; self-care is a temporary pleasure.

Once you recognize your center, it will be so open and full of deep wisdom you could never have imagined.

Here's some great advice I'll share with you that I wish someone would have told me when I was younger:

> _"If you expect nothing from somebody you are never disappointed."_
> — **Sylvia Plath, The Bell Jar**

My interpretation of that is: Don't ever expect YOU from anyone else and you will never be disappointed.

Until you have created this empowering relationship with yourself, identifying your wants and needs - you can't attract like-minded people onto your wagon or into your bus.

You CAN speak about the changes you are making and be a lighthouse for others.

Chapter 17
THE JOURNEY OF BEING ATTUNED TO SELF-AWARENESS:
6-WEEK SOUL-SELF CHALLENGE

Time to grab a fresh notebook and track the path to connecting with who you are.

The following challenge is one of the many instruments I used to get started on my journey. This is such an important piece I felt called upon to create for myself and now wish to share it with you.

PLAN	*Make a plan*
PRACTICE	*Activate!*
PATIENCE	*Build your endurance*
PROGRESS	*Track your growth*
& REPEAT	*Keep going!*

This cycle is the *core* of "EVOLVE & Repeating" the process I created while moving through my own personal self-growth journey. This instrument reminds me that my self-trained disciplines will naturally take over when motivation is lacking.

This is a lifestyle strategy to form an agreement with yourself to connect inward in order to impact your life and those surrounding you. We are living in a human body with fantastic minds and beautiful souls stacked together.

Let's unite them as one and get them working in-sync.

Start with what comes naturally to your "ego self" - your human self-awareness.

#1 : PLAN

Make a Plan:
Simply make a list of the things *you want* to change or explore in life. It can be for your present or your future self.
> Examples:
>> *I want to feel good.*
>> *I want to travel.*
>> *I want to eat healthy.*
>> *I want a vacation home.*
>> *I want to quit smoking.*
>> *I want to exercise regularly.*
>> *I want to appreciate my body.*
>> *I want to connect with the love of my life.*

Make connections between the statements you wrote.

> For example:
>> *I want to eat healthy.*
>>> *I want to exercise regularly.*
>>>> *I want to appreciate my body.*

Find your bottom line - your base.

From this example list above, ultimately, I want to "feel good" is the bottom line.

Do you see the trend? The wants and needs that would follow *IF* the changes made began with →**ME**← (remember the details from our previous chapter).

We have to know WHO we are and WHAT we want in order to make changes. **EVOLVE & Repeat >>** the process. Always evolving and consciously choosing to repeat the process that got us to "level up."
Stick with me!

You may not LOVE all these new challenges and tools I'm offering. I've found that once I embraced difficult challenges it gave me a greater sense of accomplishment. Finding the JOY *throughout your journey* is KEY to living your best life.

The bottom line in my plan was to "always feel good." In order to get from one place to the next you must have discipline. The first few days or weeks of your 6-Week Soul-Self Challenge may be exciting, but you might also feel frustration. Recognize the challenges and make a conscious choice to continue to "rise up," ask yourself - what is blocking you?

Remember the commitment you made to yourself.

Make <u>no</u> exceptions or excuses for breaking the agreement you made with yourself.

If you fail, start again.

Stick to this plan we are about to explore for <u>6 weeks, 7 days a week</u> and you'll see that **anything** is possible.

#2 : PRACTICE
PRACTICE Part I: Your Physical Well-Being

1. EXERCISE
   Movement is medicine for the body and mind.
   Choose a workout that suits you- even if you don't
   like to work out, your body deserves LOVE. Yoga,
   walking, running, riding a bike, going to the gym,
   taking a hip hop class, etc.

2. JOURNAL ENTRY
   Keep a written log, calendar or notebook.
   This is part of the journey that will gain you growth
   in so many aspects of your life. Track your practice
   and your intentions daily. Before you get started
   on your workout each day, always set an intention.
   It can be very simple like:
   My intention is to release mental stressors.

   Your journal entry might look like this:
   > *DAY #1*
   > *My workout intention:*
   > *What physical exercise did I choose today:*
   > *How my workout went:*
   > *Post Workout:*
   > *My reward:*
   > *How do you feel:*
   > *What were my excuses to NOT follow through*
   > *with my commitment to myself today?*

   Keep yourself accountable.

In the midst of editing this book, posting on my Social Media is one way I choose to keep myself accountable.

My friends cheered me on and started to get inspired by my ethics and commitment to myself and my body.

PRACTICE Part II: Soul-Self Awareness

Connecting inward through daily practices begins with one word : *Gratitude.* Begin each day with written words of gratitude and end your day with words of appreciation. When we write things down, we remember them 4xs more, which makes them a repeated thought.

1. As you step out of bed in the morning speak the words *Thank You.*
2. While you sip your coffee quietly make a list of 10 things you are grateful for today. The smallest simplest things become more noticeable and valuable to you.
3. Set reminders on your phone throughout the day. 10am and 2pm : HOW AM I FEELING?

-Pause in that moment and write in your journal or in your phone notes app how you are feeling at that moment.

8am and 4pm: Reminder: I am safe and supported by the universe in every way.

Every day, when these reminders appear on your phone, speak them OUT LOUD. Let the words you read touch your heart before they touch your lips and lean into that feeling of love moving through and connecting to your body and soul, no matter what type of mood you're in- take this opportunity to reset.

As I mentioned before, I believe daily meditation is the bridge for your soul-self connection.

From standing where you are now to where you are headed.

Meditating for a short time in the early morning resets your entire day before it even begins.

I meditate regularly EVERY DAY. Usually in the mornings before anyone else rises. No matter how tired I am, how late it is or if I'm in the mood or not. I take 10-15 minutes, put on soft meditation music and listen to my breath.

Why? Because when I don't keep practicing, I recognize I'm more edgy and out of alignment throughout the day (even my family recognizes this!) Sometimes, I meditate multiple times a day.

*Instead of reaching for my phone to check email, call a friend, read text messages or social media - I **make the choice** to meditate.*

#3 : PATIENCE

It's time to outgrow your own excuses and develop a new attitude. Record moments where you found patience in your day.

Practice patience with your children, your partner, your co-workers - with yourself. Choose to avoid that quick, 'snap judgement' or negative reaction.

"*Practice the pause*" and reset your mindset.

You will notice many of these challenges will appear as <u>lessons</u> of strength and growth now that you are self-aware.

When you are committed to following through for yourself - LIFE as a whole will get easier.

> *Patience was, and still is, one of the hardest virtues for me. Being patient with myself - the timeline I had in my own head of how quickly worlds <u>should</u> be moving - was tough, and I needed to learn the essence of granting myself grace.*
>
> *I needed to look at myself in the mirror and slow down my thoughts.*
>
> *I consistently had dozens of internet tabs open in my brain at a time and it was overwhelming, to say the*

least. I wanted things to happen in an instant, right when I wanted them to happen. In the past when they didn't, I'd throw in the towel. (This action was a choice and an <u>excuse</u> to stop moving onward and stunted my own growth).

I learned to embrace that my greatest challenge in life is practicing patience.

For example - The 'law of attraction' was calling me to live in the feeling of having that thing for which I most longed - <u>that feeling of constant joy</u>.

Through practice, meditation and all of these exercises in this book, I finally surrendered - got out of my own way - trusting the timing of the universe. I found joy in the journey through having patience.

I began to pay attention to small victories and not harp on timelines. For example, walking my dogs in freezing cold 19-degree weather. I do not like the cold. Though I was born on the last day of the year, I am a summer girl.

When I'd complain about how cold it was, it felt even colder! I was cold all the time because I kept complaining it was cold. The moment I took my dogs for a walk and consciously stopped paying attention to the weather and started to notice the world around me, my mindset shifted and so did my body temperature.

Walking my dogs gave them the exercise they needed, got them and me out of the house to bond, to experience the fresh air, the beautiful sky, the birds – red, blue and brown - that surrounded me. Walking the dogs in any kind of weather gave me clarity. I put my phone in my pocket and silenced it. I dedicated that time to myself, nature and my dogs. While it was still 19 degrees outside, I took back my power.

I stopped trying to hurry them up and learned the importance of our walks together. I made a choice to release myself from having to have control. I practiced patience. And if I was really tight on time, then I chose to start my day earlier. I found this was a better version because, everything I wanted to do, was able to be done. And even better, it kept my mind from running as if I were on a treadmill. I was able to be true to myself in my commitment I made to better my life.

#4 : PROGRESS

Record those moments where you made progress.

Victorious moments are milestones in your progress!

Progress is measured by: YOU!

Not by your friends, not by your partner, not by anyone on social media - (not even by me!).
It is measured by YOU.

Once you have done all of the exercises for SIX weeks, SEVEN days a week - in the *6-Week Soul-Self Challenge*, give yourself a review.

> *Where did I make progress?*
> *How do I feel?*
> *Where did I slack off?*
> *What habits - good and bad did I obtain?*

>> **Yes! track those bad habits too, because in order to know where you are going, you need to know where you came from and not ignore it.*

Progress needs an affirmation attached.

Put a post-it note on your mirror, write in your journal or on your calendar and speak these words every single day.

> *I AM exercising regularly.*
> *I AM eating healthier.*
> *I AM feeling good.*
> *I AM making great choices.*

#5 : REPEAT>>

If you're feeling like you don't have the time for this *6-Week Soul-Self Challenge*, I'd urge you to **_make_** the time. This challenge became a life altering program for my clients who finally choose to make themselves a priority. They were either sick of being taken advantage of and unhappy with who they were inside at times. Others wanted to seek out that inner passion and desired to connect fully with their 'soul-self.'   My INTUITIVE POWER LIFE COACHING gave them the accountability, support and strength they needed to seek JOY and happiness for their long term, future self and the future of their lineage and so on.

I am here for you.

We make time for the important things we want in life and if you want even a slice of aligning with your soul-self - you need this!

What could be more important than exploring your own personal self-growth journey to fall in love with your life!?

Lay one brick at a time - one day at a time - creating a path to walk upon to EVOLVE into the next best version of yourself. That path you're building upon for yourself becomes a paved road for others to pursue in their own journey.

You may be an inspiration for another to seek and want more for themselves, too.

Never feel ashamed if you drifted off the path or agreement you promised.

Learn to *live in the present:* don't look back with heartache or remorse and don't look forward with worry or apprehension.

Never regret one day of your past.
It's your past, those *twists and turns* that got you here- your present - to pick up this book.

You are here now! Seeking, soul-searching, wanting MORE for yourself and those around you.

Let's pretend it's been a full 6 weeks and you've completed the *6-Week Soul-Self Challenge:*

> *You set a plan to exercise 7 days a week for 6 weeks straight. To meditate 7 days a week at least once a day, to journal daily, record your habits, achievements and setbacks.*

NOW WHAT?
Write yourself a THANK YOU LETTER at the end of that 6-week journey and then **KEEP GOING** FORWARD

REPEAT>>!

> Why would you stop? Look how far you've come! Be excited, share your growth and breakthroughs with others!

> > Go back to that original list of your *wants.* Choose something new on that list (to add to your current routine) and commit to it for 6 weeks: crush *that* goal, too!

You have now propelled to the next level of identifying with self-discipline, strength, mindset and goal-digging. You didn't give up and here you are - **EVOLVE>>D**!

By choosing to **REPEAT>>** the process, you are intentionally moving forward; opening more and more to deepen the connection to your soul-self.

You are on the bridge
Keep walking.

Chapter 18

WIDEN YOUR LENS

There are going to be days, even weeks at a time, where you may feel disconnected. As if you lost that connection to the path of your soul-self you worked so hard to gain.

Maybe you are dealing with struggles, disappointments, grief, anxiety, fear or are feeling depressed.

That's OKAY; it happens to all of us.

Be kind to yourself and FEEL those feelings. Acknowledge them and accept it's "okay to not be okay."   That's being human and THIS is exactly why you are working towards the ability to step into your
soul-self!

We can't avoid these universal ebbs and flows, but we can recognize when this flow is occurring. We can choose to re-center ourselves now that we have been **"Broken Open."**

You <u>can</u> give yourself 10 minutes to jump, scream, cry and feel sorry for yourself. You have put strength and practice into your space and have the wisdom to know and control your own power that enables you to **reconnect** to your soul-self again.

You have experienced the "already, always-knowing" of coming back to your center: that stillness and peace that lies inside you. You hold that power to overcome any storm that's occurring, recognizing this storm will eventually run out of rain.

When this happens, listen to your body and rest. Go with the universal flow and let it be. No matter what happens you can change your mindset and choose joy, even on your darkest of days. You can choose to dive back into chapters in this book and work on areas to pull yourself out of the rut.

No matter what, don't beat yourself up if you're not transitioning as fast as you think you should.

YOUR growth is your own; it will happen at the pace that is right for YOU - in the time it is meant to occur.

Have patience.

Chapter 19
MY SEND OFF...
NOW SPREAD YOUR WINGS!

I'm hopeful you have experienced some "aha" moments along the way; such a profound sense of ease, excitement and peace inside of you - strengthened to embrace life and incorporate all of these insights into *every* day, in *every* way!

You may even feel so passionate that you want to tell everyone around you about this amazing insight you found in this book.

By the tiniest shifts you make, you sow the seeds you are planting for your future self, your children and those surrounding you.

There is space enough for <u>all</u>:
    to have more,
        to be connected with our soul-selves,
            and
                to live our best,
                        most-deserved,
                              loved lives.

Celebrate the joyful moments, those "God-winks," throughout your journey.

YOU are an example and making an impact for others to *open the door* to their own life-discovery - their personal self-growth journey.

Take accountability for your life. Everything you think, want and speak **will** be, if you are choosing it.

It's about living a life of LOVE *intentionally*, no matter what road you choose.

I hope the light inside of you brightens - shining onto others.

The Love inside of me honors the Love inside of you. "My soul-self honors your soul-self."

May *you choose* to be BROKEN OPEN, too.

Happy Beginnings,

Aubrey ♡

Love the Love

WORKS CITED

Bernstein, Gabrielle. *The Universe Has Your Back*
     https://gabbybernstein.com

Byrne, Rhonda. *The Secret : The 10th Anniversary Edition.*
     New York, Ny, Atria Books ; Hillsboro, Or, 2016.

Hicks, Esther, and Jerry Hicks. *Money, and the Law of*
     Attraction : Learning to Attract Wealth, Health,
     and Happiness. Carlsbad, Calif., Hay House, 2

http://abrahamhicks.com

"If you expect nothing from somebody you are never disappointed." — **Sylvia Plath, The Bell Jar**

Chakra Picture: Photo Credit: Pinterest: La Vie en Orange | korijock.com

"On Children" Kahlil Gibran, author of The Prophet

"Be the change that you wish to see in the world."
                              — *Mahatma Gandhi*

February 25, 2021 My Instagram Read...

DONE by 8am.
Giving →ME← the attention
"MY" body & mind need to live
a life full of JOY&LOVE.
If that means sacrificing an
extra hour or 2 of sleep so be
it.

5am : Shower
5:15 : Meditation & Yoga
6am : Feed the dogs
Fill every diffuser
Coffee

PRACTICE =Self Reflection
WRITTEN WORDS of GRATITUDE.

6:30-7:30 INTENTIONAL to my children, caring & prepping
their day.
Including going OUTSIDE to watch the SUNRISE & giving
appreciation in those moments to the universe.
Then tossed a load of laundry in.

7:30-8am Cardio & Strength.
Maybe a bike ride on my Peloton or an insane CRyanFit
workout.
Getting out the crazy mental stressors AND giving MY body
the LOVE it deserves, strength & soul.
laundry now in the dryer.
(So I can rock my Bikini this summer feeling confident for NO
ONE else but "ME") & because I LOVE FEELING GREAT!

And by the way-My kids are virtual today.

And my husband's been traveling all week.
I have a 9am meeting for 2 hours with my editor.

I need to walk the dogs and a million things to do following.
I don't "have it easy" I WORK at myself EVERY SINGLE DAY

And before my editor meeting this morning the laundry will
be folded and put away.

I own a dance studio
I'm finalizing a book that's taken me 2 years to write.
I have 2 kids, a super supportive husband,
a life coaching business
AND I'm taking a 90 day business education course.

Point being: "We all have stuff" & no one's life is "busier or
better" than another's.
What we have are CHOICES!
This morning could have been chaotic.

But I CHOOSE every single day DISCIPLINE to live a life heart
forward* HAPPINESS & it feels so good.
It all begins with ME.
NO ONE ELSE BUT ME!

You can choose to drown in your own personal self-
destructive or WANT MORE!
Seek out opportunities to do
WHATEVER IT TAKES to better YOURSELF.

STOP making EXCUSES for the
"why you can't" in life.
When it comes to
YOUR actions,
YOUR health,
YOUR words : present and past.
YOU woke up today= Choose to start again.

More life coaching advice, workshops and 1:1 follow my page
@aubreyconley_lifecoach on Instagram
www.aubreyconley.com

WITH DEEP APPRECIATION

♥ Thank you to my beautiful son, Chase Jonathan Conley. You are a gift from heaven, sent to teach your Momma patience, unconditional love and a strength I never knew existed inside of me. Thank you for creating this gorgeous book cover that I love and will always cherish. I pray you always lean into your 'soul-self' and inspire others to do the same. Know you are never alone and always protected by God and your angels. I pray you always follow your heart and be pulled toward those who feel like the sun. I love you dister mister- you are my heart of gold.

♥ My sweet Ava Love Aubrey Conley. You are my favorite girl in the whole wide world, the picture of perseverance who holds pure love and peace for all things, nature, animals and humanity. Your life's journey and purpose is an incredible example to everyone and everything that comes in your path. You completed our family of four, I prayed for you and God delivered. Thank you for your beautiful, inspirational photography on the cover and throughout Momma's book. You inspire me every day and I have learned so much from you. I pray you always lean into your 'soul-self' and know you are forever connected with your angels, God and all 'divine-ness'. To my Petunia Pot: I love you dister sister – you are my soul-mate .

WITH DEEP APPRECIATION

♥ Thank you to my love, my number one fan and support system: my husband, Jonathan Conley. For your encouragement in supporting me to speak my truths. For embracing me in seeking and connecting to my best, truest self, my 'soul-self' every day. For your unconditional love, spoken truths, gentle pushes and pulls of support. Your peaceful presence - I am grateful for you -investing all of you in all of me - always. I'm in love with you. I love you forever in this lifetime and the next. And when it's time to *start again*, I know we will find one another. Keep evolving, keep expanding, lean into the highest good for all, into your 'soul-self' always. Xo Ever the Same.

♥ Thank you to my best friend since the 7th grade and talented artist Effie Cardwell. You drew my beautiful spirit animal for this book, my dear white owl. Thank you for your unconditional friendship, love and support. For always going beyond any limitations, for always showing up, supporting me, lifting me up and always standing up for me, even when I am wrong. The ying to my yang.

♥ Thank you to my dear friend, editor, my 'sheriff' - Denise Maggetti Nowak. You have kept me on my toes for years and continue to do so with your wisdom and loving guidance. I have genuinely *loved* every moment working with you in editing my book. It has become more than I ever imagined. Your attention to detail and knowing *me for me*...has made this journey that much more beautiful. I am forever grateful.

♥ Rachel Markey Photography : For your beautiful photography of myself and my family found throughout my book. I love your eye for artistry and compassion for life. I am forever grateful and will cherish these captured moments in time.

With Deep Appreciation

♥ For those whose paths I've crossed -whether for a moment, a lesson or a lifetime. I am grateful for the good, the bad, the ugly and naked truths unveiled that I learned to surrender; the silver-linings that strengthened me to look inward and step into my power.

♥ To those who started out as friends then became our chosen family. Thank you for choosing me and mine. The beautiful humans who have ran to our rescue in the middle of the night, who have lent a hand, a sleepover, a hammer, held up our floors and walls physically and supportingly without hesitation. Thank you for taking on my kids, my husband and me. For showing up, not just at events and never by obligation - but always a constant in my family's life, woven and spun together - unconditionally.

For cheering me on and telling me how proud you are of me for writing this book and speaking my truths! Old friends, new friends and my family. I am grateful.

Those who have trudged through the mud, listened to my cries while handing me a tissue, glass of wine and a hug. To each of you- my beautiful chosen family and friends, I genuinely cherish and thank you. I didn't want to forget any names. If this touched you, yes... it's YOU!

ABOUT THE AUTHOR
AUBREY LYNN CONLEY

MOMMA, WIFE, DANCE STUDIO OWNER
WELLNESS ADVOCATE, INTUITIVE POWER LIFE COACH AND AUTHOR

It all started when... I began teaching children to dance. The joy and happiness it brought to their eyes, how their body language changed. I knew instantly I was watching their hearts speak. It was then I knew my purpose in this life was bigger than me. Bigger than teaching dance.

Serving humanity has led me down many different avenues in my life and professional career. The one bottom line and common factor has always been... people. I love seeing humans happy. Guiding those to look inward, releasing self-judgment and judgements of others- beautiful transformations happen. When people surrender the weight carried on their shoulders, surrender feeling offended by others' life choices and implement an attainable roadmap to reach high for their own goals. Amazing fruit blossoms in all directions in your path. Suddenly, everything in life becomes easier. I LOVE seeing people happy. I LOVE supporting others in finding themselves and their true happiness.

AUBREY CONLEY : L I F E C O A C H www.aubreyconley.com